The
Art of Fiction
&
Modern Fiction

VIRGINIA WOOLF

RENARD PRESS

RENARD PRESS LTD

124 City Road
London EC1V 2NX
United Kingdom
info@renardpress.com
020 8050 2928

www.renardpress.com

The Art of Fiction first published in 1947
Modern Fiction first published in 1925
This edition first published by Renard Press Ltd in 2024

Edited text, selection and notes © Renard Press Ltd, 2024
Cover design by Will Dady

Printed on FSC-accredited papers in the UK by 4edge Limited

ISBN: 978-1-80447-126-5

9 8 7 6 5 4 3 2 1

CONTENTS

THE ART OF FICTION

THAT FICTION IS A LADY, and a
lady who has somehow got herself
into trouble, is a thought that must
often have struck her admirers. Many gallant
gentlemen have ridden to her rescue, chief
among them Sir Walter Raleigh and Mr Percy
Lubbock.* But both were a little ceremonious in
their approach; both, one felt, had a great deal
of knowledge of her, but not much intimacy
with her. Now comes Mr Forster,* who disclaims
knowledge but cannot deny that he knows the
lady well. If he lacks something of the others'
authority, he enjoys the privileges which are
allowed the lover. He knocks at the bedroom
door and is admitted when the lady is in slippers
and dressing gown. Drawing up their chairs to
the fire they talk easily, wittily, subtly, like old

friends who have no illusions, although in fact the bedroom is a lecture room and the place the highly austere city of Cambridge.

This informal attitude on Mr Forster's part is of course deliberate. He is not a scholar; he refuses to be a pseudo-scholar. There remains a point of view which the lecturer can adopt usefully, if modestly. He can, as Mr Forster puts it, 'visualise the English novelists not as floating down that stream which bears all its sons away unless they are careful, but as seated together in a room, a circular room – a sort of British Museum reading room – all writing their novels simultaneously'. So simultaneous are they, indeed, that they persist in writing out of their turn. Richardson insists that he is contemporary with Henry James. Wells will write a passage which might be written by Dickens.* Being a novelist himself, Mr Forster is not annoyed at this discovery. He knows from experience what a muddled and illogical machine the brain of a writer is. He knows how little they think about methods; how completely they forget their grandfathers; how absorbed they tend to become in some vision of their own. Thus, though the scholars have all his respect, his sympathies are with the untidy and harassed people who are scribbling away at their books. And looking down on them, not from any great height, but, as he says, over their shoulders, he makes out, as he passes, that certain shapes and ideas tend to recur in their minds whatever their period. Since storytelling began stories have always been made of much the same elements; and these, which he calls the Story, People, Plot, Fantasy, Prophecy, Pattern and Rhythm,* he now proceeds to examine.

Many are the judgements that we would willingly argue, many are the points over which we would willingly linger, as Mr Forster passes lightly on his way. That Scott* is a storyteller and nothing more; that a story is the lowest of literary organisms; that the novelist's unnatural preoccupation with love is largely a reflection of his own state of mind while he composes – every page has a hint or a suggestion which makes us stop to think or wish to contradict. Never raising his voice above the speaking level, Mr Forster has the art of saying things which sink airily enough into the mind to stay there and unfurl like those Japanese flowers which open up in the depths of the water. But greatly though these sayings intrigue us, we want to call a halt at some definite stopping place; we want to make Mr Forster stand and deliver. For possibly, if fiction is, as we suggest, in difficulties, it may be because nobody grasps her firmly and defines her severely. She has had no rules drawn up for her, very little thinking done on her behalf. And though rules may be wrong and must be broken, they have this advantage – they confer dignity and order upon their subject; they admit her to a place in civilised society; they prove that she is worthy of consideration. But this part of his duty, if it is his duty, Mr Forster expressly disowns. He is not going to theorise about fiction except incidentally; he doubts even whether she is to be approached by a critic, and if so, with what critical equipment. All we can do is to edge him into a position which is definite enough for us to see where he stands. And perhaps the best way to do this is to quote, much summarised, his estimates of three great figures – Meredith, Hardy and Henry James.* Meredith is an exploded philosopher. His vision of nature is 'fluffy and lush'. When he gets serious and noble he becomes a bully. 'And his novels; most of the social values are faked. The tailors are not tailors, the cricket matches are not cricket.' Hardy is a far greater writer. But he is not so successful as a novelist because his characters are 'required to contribute too much to the plot; except in their rustic humours their vitality has been impoverished, they have gone thin and dry – he has emphasised causality more strongly than his medium permits'. Henry James pursued the narrow path of aesthetic duty and was successful. But at what a sacrifice? 'Most of human life has to disappear before he can do us a novel. Maimed creatures can alone breathe in his novels. His characters are few in number and constructed on stingy lines.'

Now if we look at these judgements, and place beside them certain admissions and omissions, we shall see that if we cannot pin Mr Forster to a creed we can commit him to a point of view. There is something – we hesitate to be more precise – which he calls 'life'. It is to this that he brings the books of Meredith, Hardy or James for comparison. Always their failure is some failure in relation to life. It is the humane as opposed to the aesthetic view of fiction. It maintains that the novel is 'sogged with humanity'; that 'human beings have their great chance in the novel'; a triumph won at the expense of life is in fact a defeat. Thus we arrive at the notably harsh judgement of Henry James. For Henry James brought into the novel something besides human beings. He created patterns which, though beautiful in themselves, are hostile to humanity. And for his neglect of life, says Mr Forster, he will perish.

But at this point the pertinacious pupil may demand: 'What is this "Life" that keeps on cropping up so mysteriously and so complacently in books about fiction? Why is it absent in a pattern and present in a tea party? Why is the pleasure that we get from the pattern in *The Golden Bowl** less valuable than the emotion which Trollope* gives us when he describes a lady drinking tea in a parsonage? Surely the definition of life is too arbitrary, and requires to be expanded.' To all of this Mr Forster would reply, presumably, that he lays down no laws; the novel somehow seems to him too soft a substance to be carved like the other arts; he is merely telling us what moves him and what leaves him cold. Indeed, there is no other criterion. So, then, we are back in the old bog; nobody knows anything about the laws of fiction; or what its relation is to life; or to what effects it can lend itself. We can only trust our instincts. If instinct leads one reader to call Scott a storyteller, another to call him a master of romance; if one reader is moved by art, another by life, each is right and each can pile a card-house of theory on top of his opinion as high as he can go. But the assumption that fiction is more intimately and humbly attached to the service of human beings than the other arts leads to a further position which Mr Forster's book again illustrates. It is unnecessary to dwell upon her aesthetic functions because they are so feeble that they can safely be ignored. Thus, though it is impossible to imagine a book on painting in which not a word should be said about the medium in which a painter works, a wise and brilliant book, like Mr Forster's, can be written about fiction without saying more than a sentence or two about the medium in which a novelist works. Almost nothing is said about words. One might suppose, unless one had read them, that a sentence means the same thing and is used for the same purposes by Sterne* and by Wells. One might conclude that *Tristram Shandy* gains nothing from the language in which it is written. So with the other aesthetic qualities. Pattern, as we have seen, is recognised, but savagely censured for her tendency to obscure the human features. Beauty occurs but she is suspect. She makes one furtive appearance – 'beauty at which a novelist should never aim, though he fails if he does not achieve it' – and the possibility that she may emerge again as rhythm is briefly discussed in a few interesting pages at the end. But for the rest fiction is treated as a parasite which draws sustenance from life and must in gratitude resemble life or perish. In poetry, in drama, words may excite and stimulate and deepen without this allegiance; but in fiction they must first and foremost hold themselves at the service of the teapot and the pug dog, and to be found wanting is to be found lacking.

Strange though this unaesthetic attitude would be in the critic of any other art, it does not surprise us in the critic of fiction. For one thing, the problem is extremely difficult. A book fades like a mist, like a dream. How are we to take a stick and point to that tone, that relation, in the vanishing pages, as Mr Roger Fry* points with his wand at a line or a colour in the picture displayed before him? Moreover, a novel in particular has roused a thousand ordinary human feelings in its progress. To drag in art in such a connection seems priggish and cold-hearted. It may well compromise the critic as a man of feeling and domestic ties. And so while the painter, the musician and the poet come in for their share of criticism, the novelist goes unscathed. His character will be discussed; his morality, it may be his genealogy, will be examined; but his writing will go scot-free. There is not a critic alive now who will say that a novel is a work of art and that as such he will judge it.

And perhaps, as Mr Forster insinuates, the critics are right. In England, at any rate, the novel is not a work of art. There are none to be stood beside *War and Peace*, *The Brothers Karamazov* or *À la recherche du temps perdu.** But while we accept the fact, we cannot suppress one last conjecture. In France and Russia they take fiction seriously. Flaubert* spends a month seeking a phrase to describe a cabbage. Tolstoy writes *War and Peace* seven times over. Something of their pre-eminence may be due to the pains they take, something to the severity with which they are judged. If the English critic were less domestic, less assiduous to protect the rights of what it pleases him to call life, the novelist might be bolder too. He might cut adrift from the eternal tea table and the plausible and preposterous formulas which are supposed to represent the whole of our human adventure. But then the story might wobble; the plot might crumble; ruin might seize upon the characters. The novel, in short, might become a work of art.

Such are the dreams that Mr Forster leads us to cherish. For his is a book to encourage dreaming. None more suggestive has been written about the poor lady whom, with perhaps mistaken chivalry, we still persist in calling the art of fiction.

MODERN FICTION

I N MAKING ANY SURVEY, even the freest and loosest, of modern fiction, it is difficult not to take it for granted that the modern practice of the art is somehow an improvement upon the old. With their simple tools and primitive materials, it might be said, Fielding did well and Jane Austen* even better, but compare their opportunities with ours! Their masterpieces certainly have a strange air of simplicity. And yet the analogy between literature and the process, to choose an example, of making motor cars scarcely holds good beyond the first glance. It is doubtful whether in the course of the centuries, though we have learnt much about making machines, we have learnt anything about making literature. We do not come to write better; all that we can be said to do is to keep moving, now a little in this direction, now in that, but with a circular tendency should the whole course of the track be viewed from a sufficiently lofty pinnacle. It need scarcely be said that we make no claim to stand, even momentarily, upon that vantage ground. On the flat, in the crowd, half blind with dust, we look back with envy to those happier warriors, whose battle is won and whose achievements wear so serene an air of accomplishment that we can scarcely refrain from whispering that the fight was not so fierce for them as for us. It is for the historian of literature to decide; for him to say if we are now beginning or ending or standing in the middle of a great period of prose fiction, for down in the plain little is visible. We only know that certain gratitudes and hostilities inspire us; that certain paths seem to lead to fertile land, others to the dust and the desert; and of this perhaps it may be worthwhile to attempt some account.

Our quarrel, then, is not with the classics, and if we speak of quarrelling with Mr Wells, Mr Bennett, and Mr Galsworthy,* it is partly that by the mere fact of their existence in the flesh their work has a living, breathing, everyday imperfection which bids us take what liberties with it we choose. But it is also true that, while we thank them for a thousand gifts, we reserve our unconditional gratitude for Mr Hardy, for Mr Conrad, and in a much lesser degree for the Mr Hudson of *The Purple Land, Green Mansions,* and *Far Away and Long Ago.** Mr Wells, Mr Bennett and Mr Galsworthy have excited so many hopes and disappointed them so persistently that our gratitude largely takes the form of thanking them for having shown us what they might have done but have not done; what we certainly could not do, but as certainly, perhaps, do not wish to do. No single phrase will sum up the charge or grievance which we have to bring against a mass of work so large in its volume and embodying so many qualities, both admirable and the reverse. If we tried to formulate our meaning in one word we should say that these three writers are materialists. It is because they are concerned not with the spirit but with the body that they have disappointed us, and left us with the feeling that the sooner English fiction turns its back upon them, as politely as may be, and marches, if only into the desert, the better for its soul. Naturally, no single word reaches the centre of three separate targets. In the case of Mr Wells it falls notably wide of the mark. And yet even with him it indicates to our thinking the fatal alloy in his genius, the great clod of clay that has got itself mixed up with the purity of his inspiration. But Mr Bennett is perhaps the worst culprit of the three, inasmuch as he is by far the best workman. He can make a book so well constructed and solid in its craftsmanship that it is difficult for the most exacting of critics to see through what chink or crevice decay can creep in. There is not so much as a draught between the frames of the windows, or a crack in the boards. And yet – if life should refuse to live there? That is a risk which the creator of *The Old Wives' Tale,* George Cannon, Edwin Clayhanger, * and hosts of other figures, may well claim to have surmounted. His characters live abundantly, even unexpectedly, but it remains to ask how do they live, and what do they live for? More and more they seem to us, deserting even the well-built villa in the Five Towns, * to spend their time in some softly padded first-class railway carriage, pressing bells and buttons innumerable; and the destiny to which they travel so luxuriously becomes more and more unquestionably an eternity of bliss spent in the very best hotel in Brighton. It can scarcely be said of Mr Wells that he is a materialist in the sense that he takes too much delight in the solidity of his fabric. His mind is too generous in its sympathies to allow him to spend much time in making things shipshape and substantial. He is a materialist from sheer goodness of heart, taking upon his shoulders the work that ought to have been discharged by Government officials, and in the plethora of his ideas and facts scarcely having leisure to realise, or forgetting to think important, the crudity and coarseness of his human beings. Yet what more damaging criticism can there be both of his earth and of his Heaven than that they are to be inhabited here and hereafter by his Joans and his Peters? Does not the inferiority of their natures tarnish whatever institutions and ideals may be provided for them by the generosity of their creator? Nor, profoundly though we respect the integrity and humanity of Mr Galsworthy, shall we find what we seek in his pages.

If we fasten, then, one label on all these books, on which is one word materialists, we mean by it that they write of unimportant things; that they spend immense skill and immense industry making the trivial and the transitory appear the true and the enduring.

We have to admit that we are exacting, and, further, that we find it difficult to justify our discontent by explaining what it is that we exact. We frame our question differently at different times. But it reappears most persistently as we drop the finished novel on the crest of a sigh – Is it worthwhile? What is the point of it all? Can it be that, owing to one of those little deviations which the human spirit seems to make from time to time, Mr Bennett has come down with his magnificent apparatus for catching life just an inch or two on the wrong side? Life escapes; and perhaps without life nothing else is worthwhile. It is a confession of vagueness to have to make use of such a figure as this, but we scarcely better the matter by speaking, as critics are prone to do, of reality. Admitting the vagueness which afflicts all criticism of novels, let us hazard the opinion that for us at this moment the form of fiction most in vogue more often misses than secures the thing we seek. Whether we call it life or spirit, truth or reality, this, the essential thing, has moved off, or on, and refuses to be contained any longer in such ill-fitting vestments as we provide. Nevertheless, we go on perseveringly, conscientiously, constructing our two and thirty chapters after a design which more and more ceases to resemble the vision in our minds. So much of the enormous labour of proving the solidity, the likeness to life, of the story is not merely labour thrown away but labour misplaced to the extent of obscuring and blotting out the light of the conception. The writer seems constrained, not by his own free will but by some powerful and unscrupulous tyrant who has him in thrall, to provide a plot, to provide comedy, tragedy, love interest and an air of probability embalming the whole so impeccable that if all his figures were to come to life they would find themselves dressed down to the last button of their coats in the fashion of the hour. The tyrant is obeyed; the novel is done to a turn. But sometimes, more and more often as time goes by, we suspect a momentary doubt, a spasm of rebellion, as the pages fill themselves in the customary way. Is life like this? Must novels be like this?

Look within and life, it seems, is very far from being 'like this'. Examine for a moment an ordinary mind on an ordinary day. The mind receives a myriad impressions – trivial, fantastic, evanescent or engraved with the sharpness of steel. From all sides they come, an incessant shower of innumerable atoms; and as they fall, as they shape themselves into the life of Monday or Tuesday,* the accent falls differently from of old; the moment of importance came not here but there; so that, if a writer were a free man and not a slave, if he could write what he chose, not what he must, if he could base his work upon his own feeling and not upon convention, there would be no plot, no comedy, no tragedy, no love interest or catastrophe in the accepted style, and perhaps not a single button sewn on as the Bond Street tailors would have it. Life is not a series of gig lamps symmetrically arranged; life is a luminous halo, a semi-transparent envelope surrounding us from the beginning of consciousness to the end. Is it not the task of the novelist to convey this varying, this unknown and uncircumscribed spirit, whatever aberration or complexity it may display, with as little mixture of the alien and external as possible? We are not pleading merely for courage and sincerity; we are suggesting that the proper stuff of fiction is a little other than custom would have us believe it.

It is, at any rate, in some such fashion as this that we seek to define the quality which distinguishes the work of several young writers, among whom Mr James Joyce is the most notable, from that of their predecessors. They attempt to come closer to life, and to preserve more sincerely and exactly what interests and moves them, even if to do so they must discard most of the conventions which are commonly observed by the novelist. Let us record the atoms as they fall upon the mind in the order in which they fall, let us trace the pattern, however disconnected and incoherent in appearance, which each sight or incident scores upon the consciousness. Let us not take it for granted that life exists more fully in what is commonly thought big than in what is commonly thought small. Anyone who has read *The Portrait of the Artist as a Young Man* or, what promises to be a far more interesting work, *Ulysses*,* now appearing in the *Little Review,* will have hazarded some theory of this nature as to Mr Joyce's intention. On our part, with such a fragment before us, it is hazarded rather than affirmed; but whatever the intention of the whole, there can be no question but that it is of the utmost sincerity and that the result, difficult or unpleasant as we may judge it, is undeniably important. In contrast with those whom we have called materialists, Mr Joyce is spiritual; he is concerned at all costs to reveal the flickerings of that innermost flame which flashes its messages through the brain, and in order to preserve it he disregards with complete courage whatever seems to him adventitious, whether it be probability, or coherence, or any other of these signposts which for generations have served to support the imagination of a reader when called upon to imagine what he can neither touch nor see. The scene in the cemetery, for instance, with its brilliancy, its sordidity, its incoherence, its sudden lightning flashes of significance, does undoubtedly come so close to the quick of the mind that, on a first reading at any rate, it is difficult not to acclaim a masterpiece. If we want life itself, here surely we have it. Indeed, we find ourselves fumbling rather awkwardly if we try to say what else we wish, and for what reason a work of such originality yet fails to compare, for we must take high examples, with *Youth* or *The Mayor of Casterbridge*.* It fails because of the comparative poverty of the writer's mind – we might say simply and have done with it. But it is possible to press a little further and wonder whether we may not refer our sense of being in a bright yet narrow room, confined and shut in, rather than enlarged and set free, to some limitation imposed by the method as well as by the mind. Is it the method that inhibits the creative power? Is it due to the method that we feel neither jovial nor magnanimous, but centred in a self which, in spite of its tremor of susceptibility, never embraces or creates what is outside itself and beyond? Does the emphasis laid, perhaps didactically, upon indecency, contribute to the effect of something angular and isolated? Or is it merely that in any effort of such originality it is much easier, for contemporaries especially, to feel what it lacks than to name what it gives? In any case it is a mistake to stand outside examining 'methods'. Any method is right, every method is right, that expresses what we wish to express, if we are writers; that brings us closer to the novelist's intention if we are readers. This method has the merit of bringing us closer to what we were prepared to call life itself; did not the reading of *Ulysses* suggest how much of life is excluded or ignored, and did it not come with a shock to open *Tristram Shandy* or even *Pendennis** and be by them convinced that there are not only other aspects of life, but more important ones into the bargain.

However this may be, the problem before the novelist at present, as we suppose it to have been in the past, is to contrive means of being free to set down what he chooses. He has to have the courage to say that what interests him is no longer 'this' but 'that': out of 'that' alone must he construct his work. For the moderns 'that', the point of interest, lies very likely in the dark places of psychology. At once, therefore, the accent falls a little differently; the emphasis is upon something hitherto ignored; at once a different outline of form becomes necessary, difficult for us to grasp, incomprehensible to our predecessors. No one but a modern, no one perhaps but a Russian, would have felt the interest of the situation which Chekhov has made into the short story which he calls 'Gusev'.* Some Russian soldiers lie ill on board a ship which is taking them back to Russia. We are given a few scraps of their talk and some of their thoughts; then one of them dies and is carried away; the talk goes on among the others for a time, until Gusev himself dies, and looking 'like a carrot or a radish' is thrown overboard. The emphasis is laid upon such unexpected places that at first it seems as if there were no emphasis at all; and then, as the eyes accustom themselves to twilight and discern the shapes of things in a room we see how complete the story is, how profound, and how truly in obedience to his vision Chekhov has chosen this, that and the other, and placed them together to compose something new. But it is impossible to say 'this is comic', or 'that is tragic'; nor are we certain, since short stories, we have been taught, should be brief and conclusive, whether this, which is vague and inconclusive, should be called a short story at all.

The most elementary remarks upon modern English fiction can hardly avoid some mention of the Russian influence, and if the Russians are mentioned one runs the risk of feeling that to write of any fiction save theirs is waste of time. If we want understanding of the soul and heart, where else shall we find it of comparable profundity? If we are sick of our own materialism the least considerable of their novelists has by right of birth a natural reverence for the human spirit. 'Learn to make yourself akin to people… But let this sympathy be not with the mind – for it is easy with the mind – but with the heart, with love towards them.' In every great Russian writer we seem to discern the features of a saint, if sympathy for the sufferings of others, love towards them, endeavour to reach some goal worthy of the most exacting demands of the spirit constitute saintliness. It is the saint in them which confounds us with a feeling of our own irreligious triviality, and turns so many of our famous novels to tinsel and trickery. The conclusions of the Russian mind, thus comprehensive and compassionate, are inevitably, perhaps, of the utmost sadness.

More accurately indeed we might speak of the inconclusiveness of the Russian mind. It is the sense that there is no answer, that if honestly examined life presents question after question which must be left to sound on and on after the story is over in hopeless interrogation that fills us with a deep, and finally it may be with a resentful, despair. They are right, perhaps; unquestionably they see further than we do and without our gross impediments of vision. But perhaps we see something that escapes them, or why should this voice of protest mix itself with our gloom? The voice of protest is the voice of another and an ancient civilisation which seems to have bred in us the instinct to enjoy and fight rather than to suffer and understand. English fiction from Sterne to Meredith bears witness to our natural delight in humour and comedy, in the beauty of earth, in the activities of the intellect, and in the splendour of the body. But any deductions that we may draw from the comparison of two fictions so immeasurably far apart are futile save indeed as they flood us with a view of the infinite possibilities of the art and remind us that there is no limit to the horizon, and that nothing – no

'method', no experiment, even of the wildest –
is forbidden, but only falsity and pretence. 'The
proper stuff of fiction' does not exist; everything
is the proper stuff of fiction, every feeling, every
thought; every quality of brain and spirit is
drawn upon; no perception comes amiss. And if
we can imagine the art of fiction come alive and
standing in our midst, she would undoubtedly
bid us break her and bully her, as well as honour
and love her, for so her youth is renewed and her
sovereignty assured.

NOTES

'The Art of Fiction' was first published in *The Moment and Other Essays* (1947); 'Modern Fiction' first appeared in *The Common Reader: First Series* (1925). The text of this edition is taken in each case from the first edition, which is the authoritative text. In some instances spelling and punctuation has been silently corrected to make the text more appealing to the modern reader.

7   *Sir Walter Raleigh and Mr Percy Lubbock*: Woolf refers here to Sir Walter Alexander Raleigh (1861– 1922), an English scholar, poet and author, and is likely thinking of his literary criticism, including *The English Novel* (1894) and *On Writing and Writers* (1926). Percy Lubbock (1879–1965) was an essayist, critic and biographer, best known for his book on writing, *The Craft of Fiction* (1921).

7   *Mr Forster: Aspects of the Novel* by E.M. Forster.
     (WOOLF'S NOTE) The book Woolf alludes to
     is a 1927 collection of lectures given at Trinity
     College, Cambridge by the novelist E.M. Forster
     (1879–1970), which discusses the English
     novel, summarising what he saw as its universal
     characteristics (see first note to p. 9).

8   *Richardson... Dickens*: Forster discusses the writers
     Samuel Richardson (1689–1761), Henry James
     (1843–1916), H.G. Wells (1866–1946) and Charles
     Dickens (1812–70).

9   *Story... Pattern and Rhythm*: The seven universal
     characteristics of the novel, as highlighted by
     Forster.

9   *Scott*: That is, Sir Walter Scott (1771–1832), who
     Forster says he does 'not care for'.

10   *Meredith, Hardy and Henry James*: Woolf quotes (or
     paraphrases) passages from *Aspects of the Novel*
     in which Forster discusses the writers and poets
     George Meredith (1828–1909), Thomas Hardy
     (1840–1928) and Henry James.

12   *The Golden Bowl*: A 1904 novel by Henry James.

12   *Trollope*: That is, Anthony Trollope (1815–82), best
     known for his *Chronicles of Barsetshire* series.

14   *Sterne*: This refers to writer Laurence Sterne
     (1713–68), author of *The Life and Opinions of
     Tristram Shandy, Gentleman* (1759–67).

15   *Mr Roger Fry*: Woolf refers here to the painter
     Roger Fry (1866–1934), who was a fellow member
     of the Bloomsbury Group.

15 *War and Peace… temps perdu*: Respectively: an 1869 novel by Leo Tolstoy (1828–1910), an 1880 novel by Fyodor Dostoevsky (1821–81) and the novel usually known in English as *Remembrance of Things Past* or *In Search of Lost Time* (1913–27) by Marcel Proust (1871–1922).

15 *Flaubert*: Gustave Flaubert (1821–80), best known for his 1857 novel *Madame Bovary*, was a renowned perfectionist, declaring himself to believe in the principle of finding '*le mot juste*' ('the right word').

19 *Fielding did well and Jane Austen*: That is, writers Henry Fielding (1707–54) and Jane Austen (1775–1817).

20 *Mr Bennett, and Mr Galsworthy*: That is, the writer Arnold Bennett (1867–1931) and novelist and playwright John Galsworthy (1867–1933). Woolf had written of Bennett previously – wishing to rebut his review of her 1922 novel *Jacob's Room*, she penned a response entitled 'Mr Bennett and Mrs Brown' in 1924, laying out her ideas on modernism; later that year, Woolf's Hogarth Press published the article as the first in its *Hogarth Essays* series.

21 *Mr Conrad… Long Ago*: That is, Polish-British writer Joseph Conrad (1857–1924) and Anglo-Argentine author William Henry Hudson (1841–1922). The books referred to are *The Purple Land that England Lost: Travels and Adventures in the Banda Oriental, South America* (1885), *Green Mansions: A Romance of the Tropical Forest* (1904) and *Far Away and Long Ago: A History of My Early Life* (1918).

22 *The Old Wives' Tale... Edwin Clayhanger: The Old
    Wives' Tale* was a 1908 novel by Arnold Bennet;
    Cannon is the protagonist of his 1917 novel *Roll
    Call*; and Clayhanger is the main character in a
    trilogy: *Clayhanger* (1910), *Hilda Lessways* (1911) and
    These Twain (1916).

22 *Five Towns*: The fictional setting of Bennett's books
    – correlates to the 'Staffordshire Potteries'.

26 *Monday or Tuesday*: It is this passage that critics cite
    as giving the reasoning behind the title of Woolf's
    1921 short-story collection, *Monday or Tuesday*.

28 *Mr James Joyce... Ulysses*: Written April 1919.
    (WOOLF'S NOTE) *The Portrait of the Artist as a Young
    Man* (1916) was Joyce's first published novel; *Ulysses*
    was indeed partially serialised in *The Little Review*,
    between March 1918 and December 1920, and
    was published in book form in February 1922.

29 *Youth or The Mayor of Casterbridge*: Woolf here refers
    to Joseph Conrad's 1902 short-story collection
    Youth, a Narrative; and Two Other Stories (which con-
    tains his best-known work, *Heart of Darkness*) and
    the 1886 novel by Thomas Hardy, considered one
    of his finest works.

30 *Pendennis*: That is, *The History of Pendennis* (1848–50)
    by William Makepeace Thackeray (1811–63).

31 *Chekhov has made... 'Gusev'*: Woolf here refers to the
    1890 short story of this name by Anton Chekhov
    (1860–1904), thought to be partially based on a
    true story.

A Biographical Note on

Virginia Woolf

Adeline Virginia Stephen was born into the affluent Stephen family in Kensington on the 25th of January 1882. Woolf was the seventh of eight children in a blended family; her mother, Julia Prinsep Jackson, a Pre-Raphaelite model and philanthropist, and her father, Leslie Stephen, an author, literary critic and the first Editor of the Dictionary of National Biography, had had four children in previous marriages. Of her siblings, Virginia is the best known today, although her sister Vanessa Bell, the Modernist painter, who provided the illustrations to many of Virginia's works, is still highly thought of, and her half-brother Gerald Duckworth (from Julia's first marriage) founded the successful Gerald Duckworth and Company publishing house.

Most of the Stephen family's life was spent at their elegant town house, 22 Hyde Park Gate, as well as at the country estate, Talland House, in Cornwall, where the family visited Godrevy Lighthouse, which would eventually become the inspiration for *To the Lighthouse*. Of her childhood, Woolf wrote that she was 'born into a large connection, born not of rich parents, but of well-to-do parents, born into a very communicative, literate, letter-writing, visiting, articulate, late-nineteenth-century world', and it was in this setting that the children were given a taste of distinguished company.

Leslie Stephen's importance in the literary world and his connection to William Makepeace Thackeray (his first marriage was to the author's daughter, Harriet), as well as Julia Stephen's popularity and philanthropy, meant that the London home was frequently filled with literary royalty, including Henry James, George Meredith, Thomas Hardy and Alfred, Lord Tennyson. No doubt it was being surrounded by writers of such prowess, as well as an unfettered access to her father's impressive library, that set Woolf on the path to becoming a writer. While her parents didn't approve of education for women, they did approve of her writing, and she later described being encouraged to write 'ever since I was a little creature, scribbling a story in the manner of Hawthorne on the green plush sofa in the drawing room at St Ives while the grown-ups dined…'

Woolf spoke fondly of her early childhood – particularly of the time spent at Talland House – but was forced to grow up suddenly when, in 1895, her mother fell ill with influenza, and died in May from the complications it brought with it. The loss of her mother affected the thirteen-year-old Virginia greatly, and she suffered a mental breakdown, which marked the beginning of her suffering with mental illness.

Stella, Woolf's half-sister, returned home to take on the role of mother to Virginia and Vanessa. Two years later, however, she died, too, and Woolf was left reeling. She later wrote of this time that the family had suffered 'the lash of a random unheeding flail that pointlessly and brutally killed the two people who should, normally and naturally, have made those years not, perhaps, happy, but normal and natural.'

During this period, Woolf later said, she had also been subjected to sexual molestation by her half-brother George, from as early an age as six; it is clear that the events unsurprisingly left the young Virginia scarred.

A mere five years later, Leslie Stephen fell ill, and died soon after, in 1904, administering another blow to the young Virginia and precipitating another mental breakdown. Little about the family was recorded during this period, so not much is known about Woolf's breakdown, except that it took her about three months to recover, and it is thought that she attempted to commit suicide.

At about this time, Woolf's literary career began to take root – while she wasn't permitted to join her brothers, Thoby and Adrian, at Oxbridge universities, they introduced their sisters to their circle of friends, which included Lytton Strachey and Leonard Woolf. In the mean time, able to pursue a formal education at last, Virginia enrolled at the Ladies' Department of King's College, London, where she studied Ancient Greek, Latin and German. Her tutors, Janet Case and Clara Pater, introduced her to the women's rights movement. She also met several leading education reformists, such as the Principal of the Ladies' Department, Lilian Faithfull.

After their parents' death, Vanessa and Virginia decided to sell up and move to somewhere new. Uncertain of their financial future, they moved to 46 Gordon Square in Bloomsbury, which was a relatively cheap and bohemian area at that time. Here, they began to entertain Thoby's university friends, including writers and literary critics such as Lytton Strachey, Clive Bell and Desmond MacCarthy. The group grew in size and expanded into what became known as the Bloomsbury Set, which also included John Maynard Keynes, E.M. Forster, Roger Fry and Leonard Woolf.

Only a year later, in 1906, Thoby died; the following year, Vanessa married Clive Bell and moved out, leaving the last two siblings, Virginia and Adrian, to look for a new home. That April, they moved to 29 Fitzroy Square – not far from Gordon Square. This period was marked with difficulty, however; when travelling with Vanessa and her husband, Virginia found herself very interested in Clive Bell, and a rivalry between the sisters sprang up. Eventually, when the lease on the Fitzroy Square house ran out, she and Adrian moved to 38 Brunswick Square with John Maynard Keynes and Duncan Grant, incurring the disapproval of the Duckworth side of the family.

From July 1911, Virginia began to spend more time with Leonard Woolf, who had moved into the top floor of the Brunswick Square house. Despite her initial objections to marriage, they were wed in 1912, and moved to a new house together. During this period, Virginia continued to work on her first novel, *The Voyage Out*, while struggling with mental illness again, culminating in another suicide attempt in 1913. Leonard sought advice from medical professionals, and eventually decided that it would be best for Virginia to convalesce, so they moved to Richmond, then in the Surrey countryside, in 1914.

Over the next year, Virginia took a turn for the worse; she was still working on *The Voyage Out*, and, though having secured a promise of publication, her dread of its negative reception added to her mental unrest.

In the mean time, of course, the First World War was looming in the background, and the following year, 1916, saw the introduction of conscription. Leonard was spared on medical grounds, as he described in a letter: 'I am in great trouble about conscription. I shall, of course, apply for exemption on grounds of health – (shaking hands) and domestic hardship.' Thus the Woolfs were spared a first-hand experience of the war; none the less, it cast a shadow over much of Virginia's later work, playing an important role in the background of many of her novels.

From a young age, Virginia had enjoyed bookbinding, and she and Leonard dreamt of setting up a press of their own. In 1917 the dream became a reality: they bought a hand press, which they put on the dining-room table and began to teach themselves to make books, and founded Hogarth Press, named after their new house in Richmond. They were able to publish *Two Stories*, which contained 'The Mark on the Wall' by Virginia and 'Three Jews' by Leonard, a mere three months later. Other works soon followed, including short stories by Virginia, such as *Kew Gardens*, with woodblock illustrations by Vanessa Bell. The press soon gained traction, and they started to publish works by Clive Bell,

Roger Fry, John Maynard Keynes, T.S. Eliot, Edith Sitwell, Maxim Gorky and many more. This was a crucial step for Virginia – the means of production, of course, being tantamount to control over every aspect of her works.

In 1916 Vanessa Bell took on the Charleston Farmhouse near the Sussex coast as a summer house; it soon became the scene for a revival of the Bloomsbury Set, its members having been scattered after the war. Three years later the Woolfs followed suit, buying the Round House in Lewes, which they promptly re-sold in favour of the Monk's House in nearby Rodmell, which came with an acre of land and a view across the River Ouse towards the South Downs.

The next few years saw a great literary output from Virginia, starting with a short-story collection, *Monday or Tuesday* (1921), a novel, *Night and Day* (1922) and the novel *Jacob's Room* (1922).

It was later that year that Virginia met 'the lovely gifted aristocratic [Vita] Sackville-West', a successful writer, poet and gardener. Virginia was immediately drawn to Vita, and the two entered a relationship which would last for many years, eventually evolving into a deep friendship. Vita was good for Virginia, helping her to improve her sense of self-worth, and to see reading and writing as positive, rather than detrimental to her health, as doctors had previously suggested.

In 1924, the Woolfs moved back to Bloomsbury, taking on 52 Tavistock Square, from which they continued to run the Hogarth Press, and in which Virginia had a writing room – a room of her own. This period was also rich in literary output, and saw the publication of *Mrs Dalloway* (1925), *To the Lighthouse* (1927) and *Orlando* (1928).

It was at this point that Woolf's political ideas became more prominent: in October 1928 she gave two talks on 'women and fiction' at Newnham and Girton colleges, which led to the publication of *A Room of One's Own* the following year, and, soon after, 'Professions for Women' (1931).

Woolf now began work on her most stylistically innovative novel, *The Waves*. This was due in no small part to Vita Sackville-West publishing her books through the Hogarth Press, helping to make the press profitable and allowing Virginia to be more experimental in her writing.

In 1937, the international situation worsened again, which affected Virginia greatly – both due to her deep-set horror of war and also the death of her nephew, Vanessa's son Julian, who was killed in the Spanish Civil War. Virginia began to work on a treatise against war, *Three Guineas*, an indictment of Fascism and a portrayal of violence as a patriarchal tool.

As old friends – such as Roger Fry – died, and war loomed, her final years were darkened by tragedy. Her writing suffered as a result, as she began to doubt her abilities, but she still managed to write *Between the Acts*. In 1939 the Woolfs moved again within London, to 37 Mecklenburgh Square, but the house was destroyed during the Blitz in September 1940, so they moved permanently to Monk House in Sussex.

The couple were under immense strain – Virginia was isolated from her friends and filled with grief, and Britain feared immanent invasion by Hitler, which was all the more concerning as Leonard was Jewish. Her mental state grew worse, and on the 28th of March 1941 she filled her pockets with rocks and walked into the River Ouse, leaving a moving note to Leonard, which is now almost as well known as her books:

Dearest, I feel certain that I am going mad again. I feel we can't go through another of those terrible times. And I shan't recover this time. I begin to hear voices, and I can't concentrate. So I am doing what seems the best thing to do. You have given me the greatest possible happiness. You have been in every way all that anyone could be. I don't think two people could have been happier till this terrible disease came. I can't fight it any longer. I know that I am spoiling your life, that without me you could work. And you will I know. You see I can't even write this properly. I can't read. What I want to say is I owe all the happiness of my life to you. You have been entirely patient with me and incredibly good. I want to say that – everybody knows it. If anybody could have saved me it would have been you. Everything has gone from me but the certainty of your goodness. I can't go on spoiling your life any longer. I don't think two people could have been happier than we have been. V.

A NOTE ON SUSTAINABILITY

RENARD PRESS feels strongly that there is no denying the climate crisis, and we all have a part to play in fixing the problem.

We are proud to be one of the UK's first climate-positive publishers, taking more carbon out of the air than we put in. How? We reduce our emissions as much as possible, using green energy, printing locally and choosing the materials we use carefully; we calculate our carbon footprint and doubly offset it through gold-standard schemes; and we plant a tree for every order we receive via our website to give back to the planet.

Find out more at:

RENARDPRESS.COM/ECO

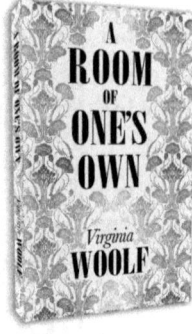

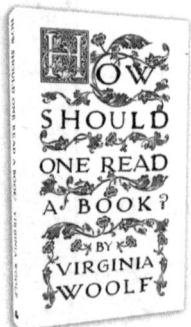
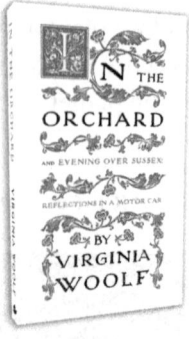